# BRAIN GAMES®

# STICKER BY NUMBER™

# FLOWERS & NATURE

## How to Sticker by Number™

Find the coordinating stickers in the back of the book to complete the picture. Place the sticker with the same code onto the matching space on the art page. Use the answer key to see the completed pages.

Brain Games is a registered trademark of Publications International, Ltd.
Sticker by Number is a trademark of Publications International, Ltd.

Louis Weber, CEO
Publications International, Ltd.
8140 Lehigh Ave
Morton Grove, IL 60053

Images from Shutterstock.com

Permission is never granted for commercial purposes.

ISBN: 978-1-64558-760-6

Manufactured in China.

8 7 6 5 4 3 2 1

**Let's get social!**
@Publications_International
@PublicationsInternational
@BrainGames.TM
www.pilbooks.com

1

3

5

9

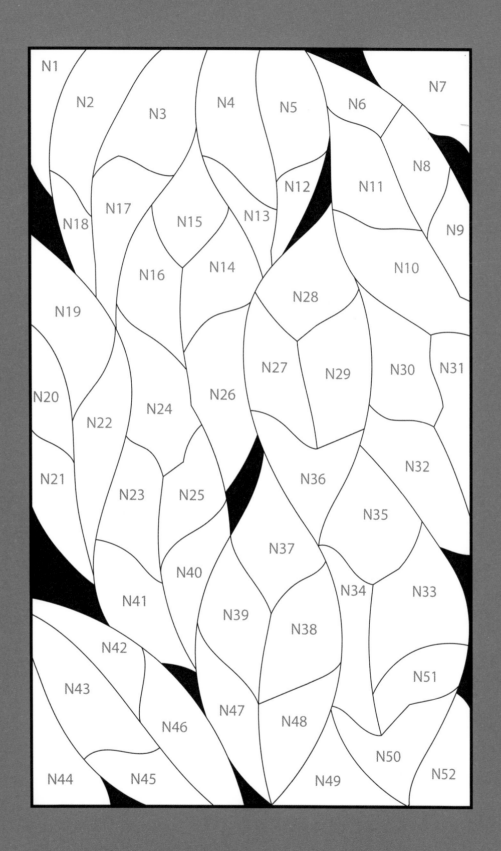

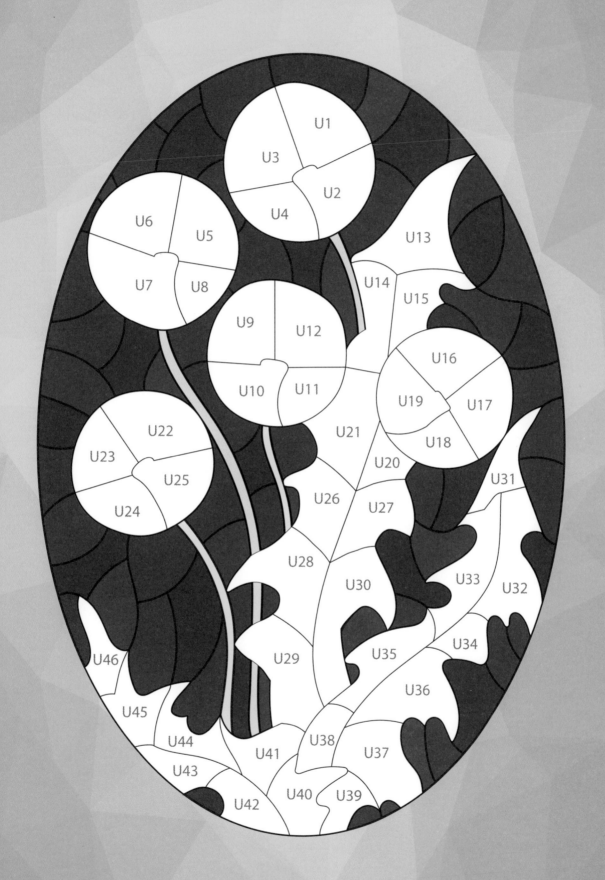

23

24

25

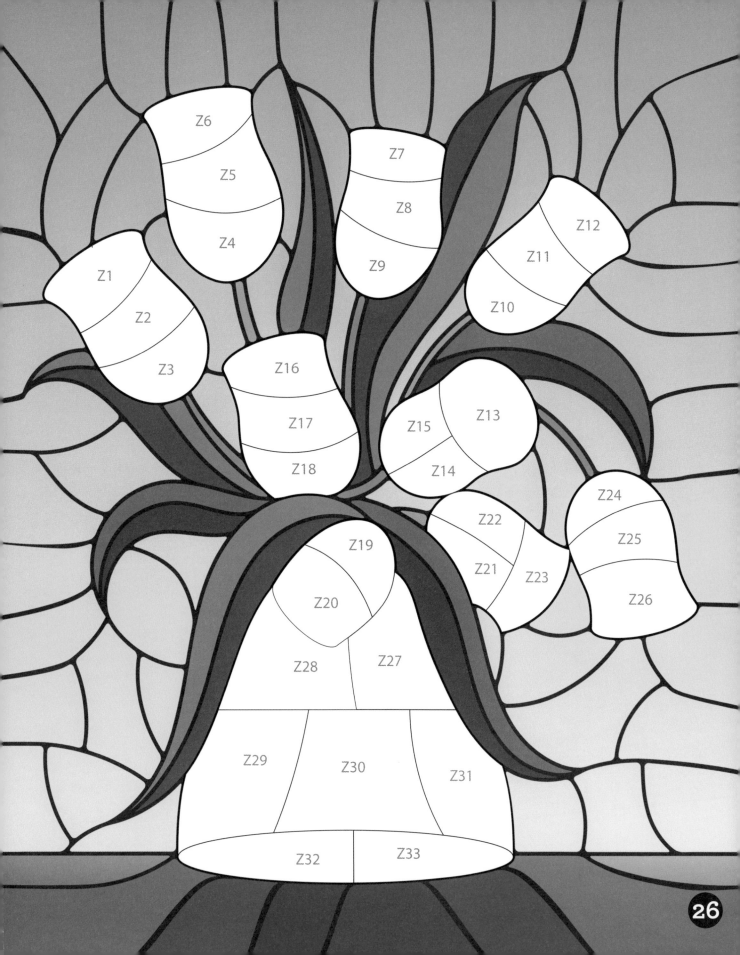

# Answer Key

**1**

**2**

**3**

**4**

**5**

**6**

**7**

**8**

**9**

**10**

**11**

**12**

13

14

15

16

17

18

19

20

**21**

**22**

**23**

**24**

25

26

27

28